"Trash to Treasure" Series
Recycling Creatively with L.T.

WEST WYANDOTTE
KANSAS CITY KANSAS
PUBLIC LIBRARY
DATE: OCT 23 2014

The Bicycle Fence

Written by Tom Noll
Illustrated by Brandon Fall

L.T. is always recycling.

Using discarded and unwanted things to create new
and useful inventions.

L.T. has been described as imaginative, resourceful and very creative.

He redesigns and transforms just about everything he gets his hands on,
making something old – New Again!

L.T. believes in reducing waste, reusing things, going green
and recycling for life to Save Our Planet.

D1074630

Think Re............
Reduce, Reuse, Recycle, Rescue, Rethink
Restore, Reinvent, Refurbish, Rebuild, Recreate
Repair, Renew, Refresh, Revive, Repurpose
Revitalize, Reimagine, Recondition, Remodel, Regenerate
Reassemble, Reorganize, Refashion, Reactivate, Rediscover

To all the dedicated and wonderful
people who recycle, go green,
protect the environment and
help save our planet for future
generations.

To you, my young readers, who
are the hopes for a better future
and a greener world for others to
enjoy, my everlasting gratitude.

To my beloved, and my friends for
their support and encouragement.
–Tom Noll ♻

To Caitlyn, Evan and Blake.
–Brandon Fall ♻

Printed on 100% Recycled (50% PCW) paper and
with eco- friendly soy ink! Proudly Made in the USA!

"Trash to Treasure" Series - Recycling Creatively with L.T.
"The Bicycle Fence" Copyright © 2014 by Tom Noll
Printed in the United States of America

Written by Tom Noll, www.LTsRecyclingWorld.com
Illustrated by Brandon Fall, www.fallillustration.com

All rights reserved. Characters, stories and websites have been trademarked.

No part of this publication may be reproduced, or stored in a retrieval system
or transmitted in any form or any means, electronic, mechanical, photocopy,
recording or other–except for brief quotations in articles or reviews, without
written permission of the publisher.

ISBN - 13: 978-1-939377-50-0
ISBN – 10: 1939377501
Library of Congress Control Number: 2013940335
UPC - 850924005007
First Edition

For information about custom editions, special sales, premium and
corporate purchases, please email us at: Alberto@greenkidspress.com

Signature Book Printing, Inc.
www.sbpbooks.com

Green Kids Press, LLC™
Nurturing Imagination & Creativity
GreenKidsPress.com

23 T Street NW – Washington, DC 20001-1008
SAN-920-458X
(202) 518-7070
Fax (202) 588-0931
Alberto@greenkidspress.com
www.GreenKidsPress.com

"Trash to Treasure" Series
Recycling Creatively with L.T.

The Bicycle Fence

Written by Tom Noll

Illustrated by Brandon Fall

Keep Recycling With L.T.

Tom Noll
2014

In the small town of Greenville, not very far away, lives a creative young boy named L.T. For L.T., an idea never stays a thought–it becomes an adventure!

L.T. used to be known as Little Tommy, but, when he outgrew his shirts, pants and shoes all in one summer, everyone started calling him L.T.

"That boy is growing faster than the weeds in our garden!" said L.T.'s dad.

L.T. also outgrew his bike—and he needed a bike to get to and from school. So, L.T.'s dad took him to "Recycleville," Mr. Salvage's junkyard and recycling center, to find one.

L.T's dad loved to recycle. He got parts for his pick-up truck from Mr. Salvage, but he never painted them to match, so his truck had a blue cab, yellow hood, red and orange doors, a green bed, and a purple tail gate. L.T. sometimes felt a little embarrassed riding in it, especially when people called out, "Here comes the junkyard truck!" He hoped his bicycle wouldn't turn out the same way.

When L.T. and his dad arrived at Recycleville, Mr. Salvage pointed out some cans of red paint and asked if they wanted to paint the truck red.

"No, thanks!" said L.T.'s dad. "I like my recycled rainbow truck!"

"One man's trash is another man's treasure!" L.T.'s dad liked to say. He said that even Rex and Sebastian, the family dog and cat, were 'recycled' – because they were rescued from the animal shelter!

L.T. had learned from his teacher, Miss White, how recycling and going green helps to save the planet.

He was proud of his dad, but he still wished he could have a brand new bike instead of a recycled one.

At home, L.T.'s dad selected one or two parts from each bike and began to connect them together. Sure enough, when he was finished, L.T.'s new bike looked just like L.T. was afraid it would look: a blue fender, red body, and green handle bars–with lots of rust. It worked well enough, but L.T. worried about riding it to school. He hoped no one would call it a 'junkyard bike.'

L.T. frowned. He needed to come up with an idea, and fast!

Mom had some white paint, so maybe he could disguise his bike! He could paint it white and call it White Lightning. The white was for Miss White, because she was so nice, and the lightning because it was fast, just like L.T. would be on his "new" bike.

L.T. worked all weekend, carefully painting his new bike. By Monday, White Lightning was finished. Usually, he was unhappy about wearing a bicycle helmet. He knew it kept him safe, but he didn't like how it looked, so he put one of Dad's hats over it to disguise it.

L.T. felt so proud riding it to school. He had a new bike and he had helped save the planet!

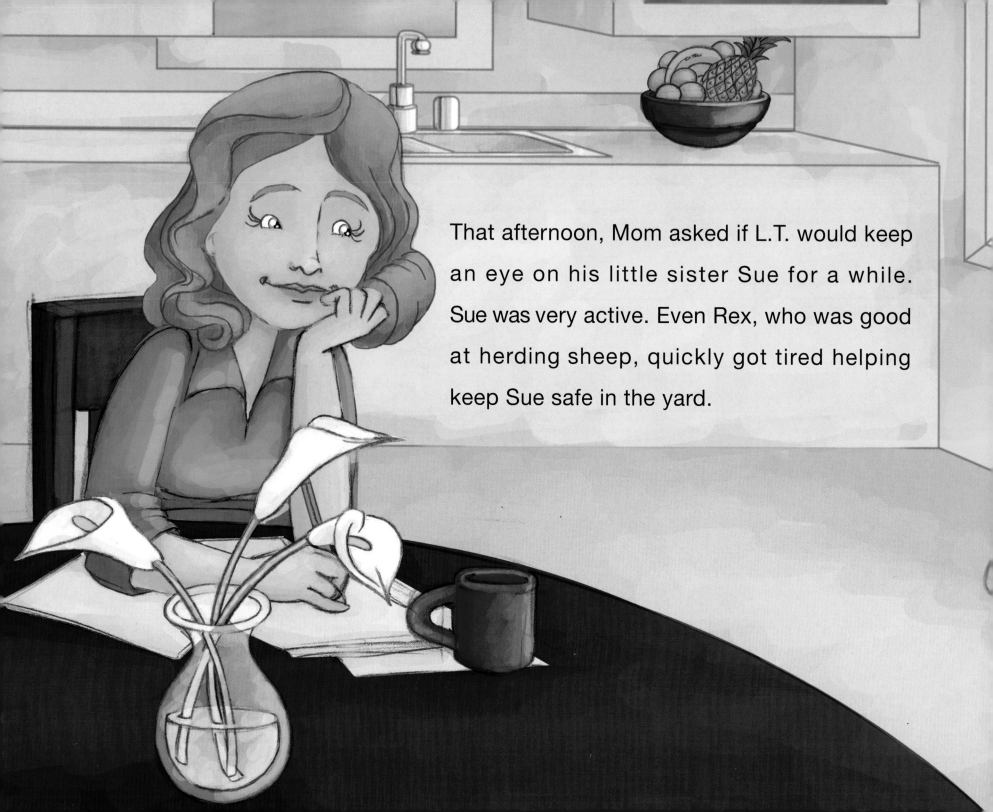

That afternoon, Mom asked if L.T. would keep an eye on his little sister Sue for a while. Sue was very active. Even Rex, who was good at herding sheep, quickly got tired helping keep Sue safe in the yard.

"If only we had a picket fence, like all the other houses on the street!" L.T. thought to himself. "Then Sue and Rex could run around all they liked, and it would be easy to keep an eye on them."

Out of the corner of his eye, he noticed the leftover bikes that he and Dad had brought home from Recycleville. That gave L.T. another idea!

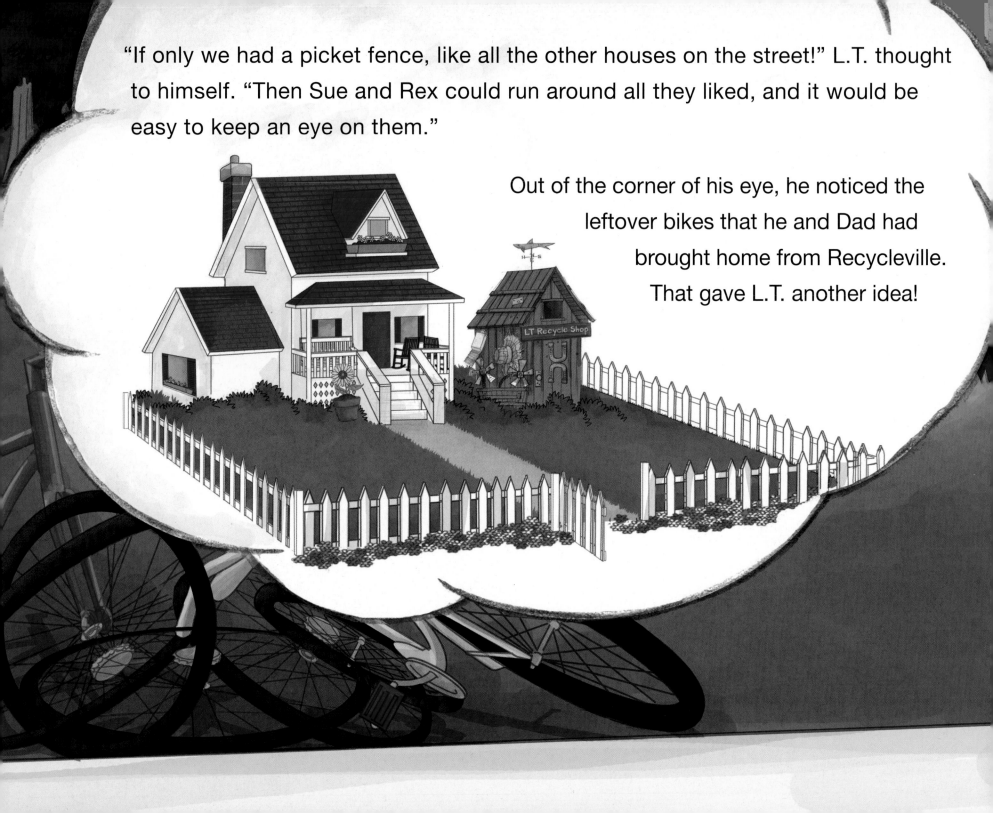

"Cow-a-bunga!" he yelled, and ran to his bedroom.

He grabbed a pile of clothes he had outgrown,

and ran back out to the yard.

He lined up all the leftover and outgrown bikes. Then, one by one, he tied them together using his old shirts, socks, pants, and a belt.

Next day L.T. with his dad lined up
and secured all the bikes in the front
of the house to create a fence. Then he
painted them all white with the leftover paint.

When he was done, L.T. looked at his
new white fence with pride.

Old Mr. Smith, the neighbor, called out,
"Nice fence, L.T.!"

"Thanks!" L.T. replied.
"One man's trash is my treasure!"

This has been the greatest summer.

L.T. likes to think about all the adventures he will have

creatively recycling and saving the planet!

The all-grown-up L.T. has his own recycled rainbow truck
and white bicycle fence.

Tom Noll, Author

Tom is an artist, sculptor, landscape designer, avid nature lover, recycler and advocate for going green. Tom is a native of Somerset, Ohio and is a first time writer who lives in the Washington, D.C. metropolitan area. For the 15 years that he lived in Manassas, Virginia, he was known for his imaginative white bicycle fence at his home, which he decorated for major holidays. **www.LTsRecyclingWorld.com**

Brandon Fall, Illustrator

Brandon has always loved illustration and spent countless hours of his childhood getting lost in his drawings. He is now fortunate to do what he loves from his home in California. Brandon's illustration and design work has appeared in a number of publications. He enjoys spending time with his wife and children in the beautiful outdoors. **www.fallillustration.com**

 # Visit www.LTsRecyclingWorld.com

… for the latest information on L.T. and his adventures in creative recycling! You and your friends can also join L.T.'s Recycling Club and take his "Recycling, Going Green & Saving the Planet Pledge." You can also print the pledge, and explore the interactive Q&A's, coloring pages and games, as well as more information, activities and adventures for kids, parents, caregivers and educators. Do send us photos of your recycling ideas or projects that you do with your family, friends, or teachers, at school or in your community. If you create your own community bicycle fence, send us photos also. We will feature them on L.T.'s website for all to learn from, admire and enjoy. You will also be able to purchase the new L.T. books when they are released:

January 2014 - **Selling Eggs** (for a winter adventure)
March 2014 - **The Flower Bed** (just in time for Mother's Day)
September 2014 - **Grandma's Garden** (learn about gardening)

Green Kids Press, LLC™
Nurturing Imagination & Creativity
GreenKidsPress.com

To Our Young Readers:

Join L.T.'s Recycling Club and take his "Recycling, Going Green & Saving the Planet Pledge" to earn your Recycling Certificate. Share the information below with your parents, grandparents, brothers, sisters, relatives, friends, teachers, and classmates. All of Us Together, doing just a couple of the things listed below, can make a big difference in Protecting Our Planet!

Things We All Can Do To Take Care and Save Our Planet Earth For Future Generations:

1. **WE can** sort and recycle trash properly in the designated bins or containers for: paper, plastic, glass, and aluminum. This way they can be reused to create new products and toys for us to enjoy.

2. **WE can** keep our homes, gardens, sidewalks, streets, schools, playgrounds, and parks clean. We can put trash in appropriate trashcans or recycle bins, and not litter our planet.

3. **WE can** plant trees, bushes, and flowers. They make the world prettier, help clean the air that we breathe, provide shade in the summer, and protect us in the winter.

4. **WE can** choose to walk, or ride a bike or use public transportation (buses, subways, trains) with an adult when going on short trips, instead of driving a car. We can share rides for longer trips with our family or friends. Cars create pollution and harm the environment.

5. **WE can** turn off lights and electronic equipment (TV, computer, stereo, air conditioner) when not in use or leaving a room. We can also unplug chargers when not charging an appliance. It will save energy and money.

6. **WE can** keep our thermostat at a reasonable temperature, and, if we get chilly, we can put on a sweater. Let's make sure our parents insulate the home and seal cracks around windows and doors; it will keep the heat inside the home.

7. **WE can** keep doors and windows closed so we do not waste air conditioning in the summer or heat in the winter. It will save energy and money.